Meteorology
For Pilots
Simplified

Captain John Swan

POOLEYS FLIGHT EQUIPMENT

All rights reserved. No part of this book may be reproduced or transmitted in any form by any means, electronic or mechanical, including photocopying, recording or by any information storage and retrieval system, without permission from the publisher in writing.

Copyright 2007 © Pooleys Flight Equipment Ltd
Meteorology for Pilots Simplified - John Swan

ISBN: 978-1-84336-133-6

Published by:
Pooleys Flight Equipment Ltd
Elstree Aerodrome
Elstree
Hertfordshire WD6 3AW

Tel: +44(0)20 8953 4870
Fax: +44(0)20 8953 2512
Email: sales@pooleys.com
Website: www.pooleys.com

Third Edition 2007
Second Edition 2001
First Edition 1995

Contents

1. **The Atmosphere.** 1
   Atmospheric composition. 1
   International Standard Atmosphere. 2

2. **Altimetry.** 3
   Vertical references. 3

3. **Stability.** 5
   Total, or absolute stability. 5
   Total, or absolute instability. 6

4. **Air Masses.** 7

5. **Pressure Systems and their Associated Weather.** 8
   High pressure. 8
       Ridge Of High Pressure. 8
   Low pressure. 9
       Trough Of Low Pressure. 9
   Col. 9

6. **Fronts.** 10
   Frontal formation. 10
   Cold front. 11
   Warm front. 11
   Occluded front. 12
   Stationary front. 12

7. **Winds.** 13
   Winds below 2,000 feet. 14
   Local winds. 15
       Land and sea breezes. 15
       Mountain waves. 15
       Fohn wind. 16
       Anabatic wind. 16
       Katabatic wind. 16

8. Clouds. ... 17
Cloud classification by altitude. ... 17
Cloud classification by shape. ... 17
Cloud formation. ... 19
    Frontal activity. ... 19
    Widespread irregular mixing of air. ... 19
    Local convection currents. ... 20
    Local orographic disturbances. ... 20
Calculation of cloud base. ... 21

9. Precipitation. ... 22

10. Thunderstorms. ... 23
Classification of thunderstorms. ... 23
    Frontal activity. ... 23
    Air mass activity. ... 23
Life cycle of thunderstorms. ... 23
    Development stage. ... 24
    Mature stage. ... 24
    Dissipation stage. ... 25
Hazards associated with thunderstorms. ... 25

11. Fog and Reduced Visibility. ... 27
Fog. ... 27
    Advection fog. ... 27
    Radiation fog. ... 28
    Hill fog. ... 28
    Frontal fog. ... 28
    Freezing fog. ... 28
Vertical and oblique visibility. ... 28

12. Icing. ... 29
Airframe icing. ... 29
    Clear ice ... 29
    Rime ice. ... 29
    Mixed or cloudy ice. ... 30
    Hoar frost. ... 30
    Preflight actions. ... 30
    In-flight actions. ... 30
Carburettor icing ... 31

13.	**Climatology.**		**32**
	Europe.		32
		Winter.	33
		Summer.	34
		Flying in Europe.	34
	North America and Canada.		35
		Winter.	35
		Summer.	36
	Australia.		37
		January.	37
		July.	38
	South Africa.		39
		January.	39
		July.	40
14.	**The Meteorological Organisation.**		**41**
	Aeronautical meteorological offices.		41
	Aerodrome meteorological offices.		41
	Meteorological services at aerodromes.		41
	Availability of periodic weather forecasts.		41
15.	**Weather Analysis and Forecasting.**		**42**
	Weather charts, symbols and signs.		42
	Prognostic charts for general aviation.		43
		Significant weather charts.	43
16.	**Weather Information for Flight Planning.**		**45**
	Reports and forecasts for departure.		45
	En-route, destination and alternate(s).		45
	Interpretation of coded information.		46
		METARs.	46
		TAFs	48
	Availability of ground reports for surface conditions.		50
	In flight meteorological information.		50
		VOLMET.	50
		ATIS.	50
		SIGMET.	50

Glossary of terms. 51

1

The Atmosphere.

The air surrounding the earth can be split into several concentric shells, the inner two being the ones that effect the earth's weather, namely the Troposphere and the Stratosphere.

The Troposphere is the air mass surrounding the earth up to an altitude of approximately 22 kilometres over the equator and 7 kilometres over the poles. It is the part of the earth's atmosphere of most interest to us as pilots, since this is the airspace we fly in, as such all the following sections of this guide refer to this part of the atmosphere unless stated otherwise.

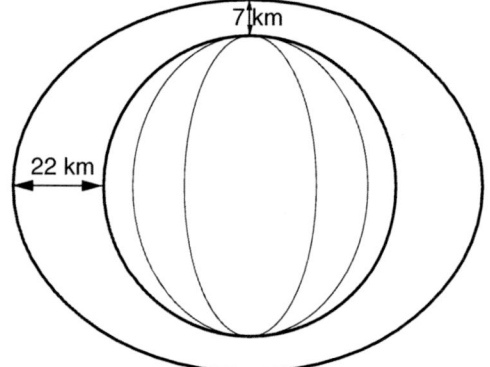

The Troposphere is separated from the surrounding Stratosphere by a layer called the Tropopause. The Stratosphere is a shell of constant temperature and strong horizontal winds.

Atmospheric composition.

The atmosphere is composed of a mixture of gases, their relative proportions remaining constant with change of altitude. The two most significant gases being, Nitrogen occupying 78% of the atmosphere and Oxygen occupying 21%, the remaining 1% consists mainly of Argon, Carbon Dioxide, Neon, Hydrogen, Ozone and Water vapour.

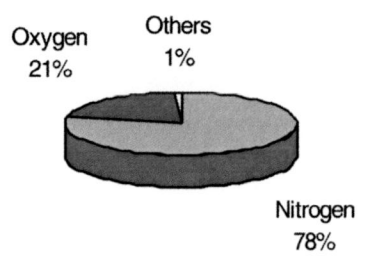

International Standard Atmosphere.

Aviation uses a standard atmosphere, which is not far removed from the average conditions for the temperate latitudes, that has been specified by the International Civil Aviation Organisation, ICAO. This is referred to as the International Standard Atmosphere, ISA, and is defined as follows:

    At mean sea level:

        Pressure   1013.25 hPa

        Temperature +15 $°C$

        Density   1225 g/m^3

    Above mean sea level the temperature varies as follows:

        Up to 36,000 ft.   Decreases by 1.98 $°C$/1,000 ft.

        From 36,000 to 65,500 ft.   Remains constant at -56.5 $°C$

The air temperature is dependant upon the temperature of the surface beneath, which by day is heated by radiation from the sun, and at night radiates into space and cools. The air in contact with the surface is either heated or cooled by conduction and mixes, by either convection or turbulence, with the air above thereby changing its temperature.

Although not covered by the International Standard Atmosphere the pressure of the air decreases at approximately 1 hPa per 30 ft. of altitude increase.

2

Altimetry.

Altimetry is the method of measurement, and display to the pilot, of the aircraft's vertical position. The altimeter is the instrument in the cockpit which displays to the pilot this information in hundreds and thousands of feet. The altimeter actually is a device that measures pressure relative to a reference pressure within the altimeter, but it is calibrated such that the dial indicates feet. The reference pressure must be adjustable to take into account different mean sea level pressures and also so the pilot can in different phases of flight use a different vertical reference.

Vertical references.

There are three standard references for vertical position:

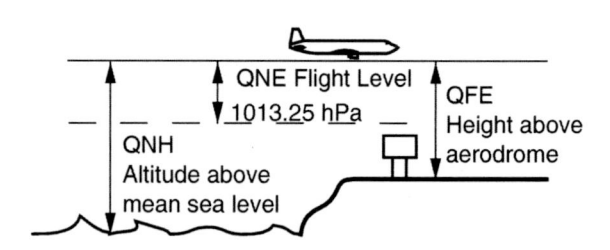

```
                    QNE Flight Level     QFE
                    1013.25 hPa          Height above
          QNH                            aerodrome
          Altitude above
          mean sea level
```

For normal low altitude VFR flights the pilots main concern with regard to vertical position is terrain clearance. In this case the altimeter is set such that it would read "0" at mean sea level, this is referred to as **QNH**. The altimeter is indicating altitude and provided an altitude greater than the heights displayed on the aviation chart are flown the aircraft will remain above the terrain. **Caution**, this assumes the air mass to which the chart relates has the same atmospheric pressure as that when the altimeter was set.

When landing at an aerodrome the pilot may find it convenient to use the airfield elevation as the reference, so the altimeter is reading the height above the airfield. This setting is referred to as **QFE**, most aerodromes now use QNH as the normal, but the pilot can request the QFE.

For flights at high altitudes and over long distances, terrain clearance is not of great concern to the pilot, of more interest is vertical separation from other traffic originating from areas that may have vary different atmospheric conditions. ICAO came up with a simple solution to this problem by setting a standard pressure reference of 1013 hPa. All aircraft above a certain altitude switch from flying with QNH as their reference to 1013 hPa and fly at what is referred to as **Flight Levels**, this altimeter setting is referred to as **QNE**.

The altitude band where an aircraft changes from QNH to 1013 hPa or vice versa is defined as follows:

Transition Altitude is the altitude below which the aircraft's vertical position is controlled by reference to altitude.

Transition Level is the lowest flight level available above the transition altitude.

Transition Layer is the layer between the transition altitude and the transition level, when descending through the layer altitude is used, and when climbing through it flight level is used.

As stated above the altimeter is a pressure sensing instrument which is calibrated to indicate the aircraft's vertical position in feet. It must be remembered that when flying level, at say 2,000 feet, you are maintaining a constant pressure, not necessarily a constant vertical position. If flying from an area of high pressure to an area of low pressure, that constant pressure line will be getting nearer to the surface but your altimeter will still be reading 2,000 feet, **it will over read**. It is of utmost importance that you reset the altimeter to the latest QNH value for your destination to ensure adequate terrain clearance.

3

Stability.

Stability in meteorological terms refers to whether a parcel of air when lifted by an external force will return to its starting altitude when that force is removed, which is stable, or whether it will continue to rise, in which case it is unstable.

Before this can be discussed in a little more detail we need to define three lapse rates, these are the rates at which air cools as it rises in the atmosphere.

>**Environmental Lapse Rate, ELR,** is the measured decrease in temperature with gain of altitude at a particular place and time.
>
>**Dry Adiabatic Lapse Rate, DALR,** is the decrease in temperature with gain of altitude, or increase with loss of altitude, of a parcel of dry air solely due to the internal pressure changes of that parcel, there is no transfer of energy from the surrounding air. This is 3 ^{0}C per 1,000 feet.
>
>**Saturated Adiabatic Lapse Rate, SALR,** is the decrease in temperature with gain of altitude of a parcel of saturated air due to expansion, partly offset by the release of energy as the moisture in the parcel of air condenses out as water droplets. Typically this is approximately 1.5 ^{0}C per 1,000 feet.

The environmental lapse rate determines the stability of an air mass since the dry and saturated adiabatic lapse rates are approximately fixed.

Total, or absolute stability.

If the environmental lapse rate is less than both the dry and saturated adiabatic lapse rates any parcel of air rising in the atmosphere will cool quicker than the surrounding air. If the lifting force is removed the parcel of air will descend to its original level.

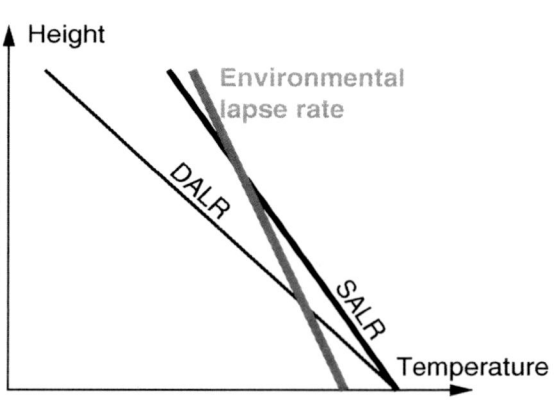

Total, or absolute instability.

If the environmental lapse rate is greater than both the dry and saturated adiabatic lapse rates any parcel of air rising in the atmosphere will cool slower than the surrounding air. Irrespective of whether the lifting force is removed or not, the parcel of air is hotter than the surroundings and will continue to rise.

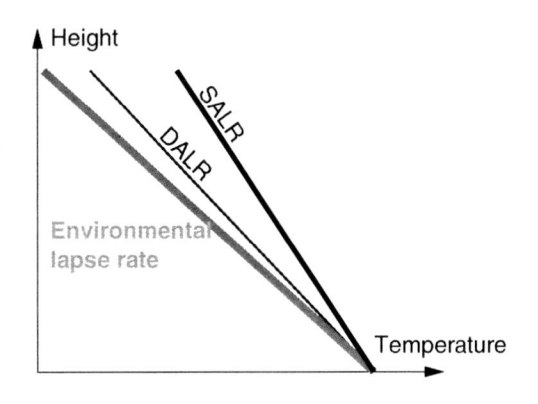

There are other cases that lie between these two limits but these are beyond the scope of this guide.

4

Air Masses.

An air mass is a large expanse of air, several hundred miles across, that has the same temperature and humidity in the horizontal plane. Air masses always form in areas of high pressure, the stability in these areas is required to get the uniformity in the horizontal plane.

Air masses are classified by their source region temperature and their humidity:

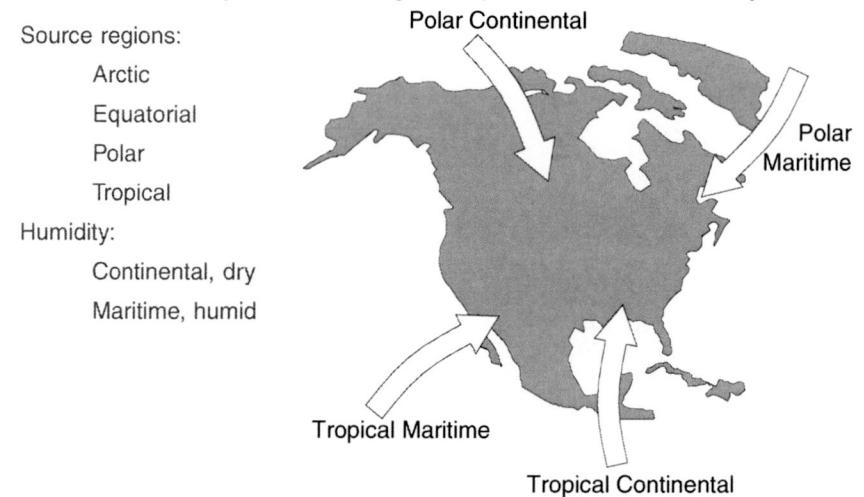

Source regions:
- Arctic
- Equatorial
- Polar
- Tropical

Humidity:
- Continental, dry
- Maritime, humid

Polar Continental

Polar Maritime

Tropical Maritime

Tropical Continental

When an air mass moves its characteristics are changed by the surface it passes over. Generally if the surface is warmer than the air mass this will lead to instability and the possibility of thunderstorm activity. If the surface is cooler than the air mass this will lead to a temperature inversion, reduced visibility in the lower atmosphere and the chance of fog and low level stratus cloud if the air mass is moist. The humidity of the air mass will increase if it passes over water.

5

Pressure Systems and their Associated Weather.

Pressure systems describe the pressure distribution over a large geographical area. There are three basic pressure systems:

    High Pressure.
    Low Pressure.
    Col.

High pressure.

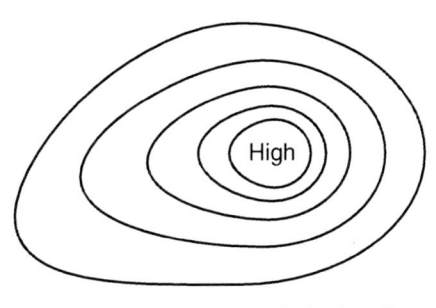

Commonly referred to as an anticyclone. A high has a higher central pressure than the surrounds, it is usually oval or circular in shape.

Highs are areas of sinking air, subsidence, adiabatic warming occurs as the air descends leading to divergence at the surface, usually resulting in stable weather. In the northern hemisphere winds blow in a clockwise direction around the high, whereas in the southern hemisphere they are anticlockwise. In either hemisphere they are normally light, the weather is good except for the possibility of fog, particularly in the winter, and haze.

Ridge Of High Pressure.

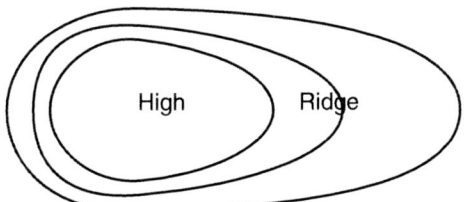

Instead of being circular in shape a ridge of high pressure protrudes out from a high having areas of lower pressure on either side.

Weather in a ridge is usually fine and clear.

Low pressure.

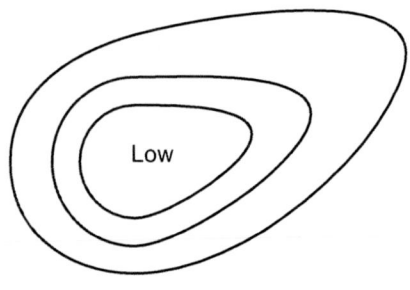

Commonly referred to as a depression. A low has a lower central pressure than the surrounds, it is usually circular in shape.

Lows are areas of ascending air, convergence occurs at the ground leading to adiabatic cooling as the air rises resulting in unstable weather. In the northern hemisphere winds blow in an anticlockwise direction around a low, whereas in the southern hemisphere they blow clockwise. Lows are usually characterised by cumulus clouds, precipitation and strong winds.

Trough Of Low Pressure.

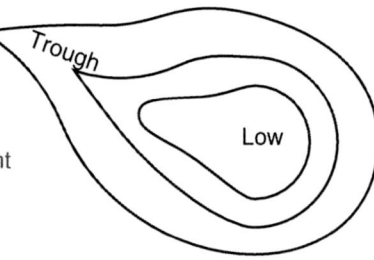

A V shaped region extending from a low, the pressure within the V being lower than that on either side.

Weather in a trough is the same as in the adjacent low.

Col.

An area bordered by two high and two low pressure regions.

Weather within a col can be anything from light winds to gales, good to bad visibility, and fine weather cumulus to towering cumulonimbus clouds.

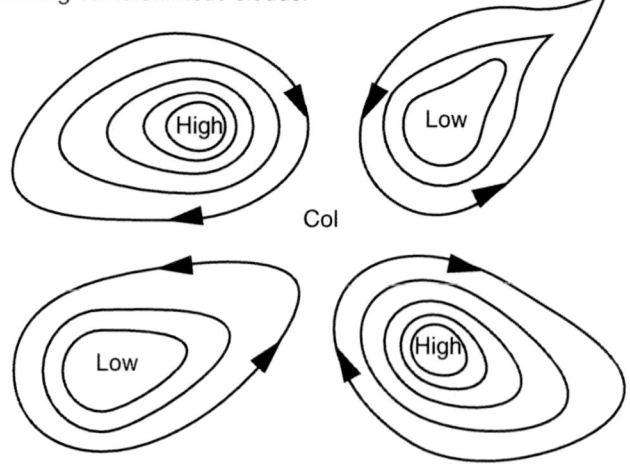

6

Fronts.

Frontal formation.

Fronts originate where two different air masses meet and a depression starts to form between them. In the northern hemisphere the warmer air pushes northwards into the colder air, forming a warm sector, of a sort of inverted curved V shape, in the southern hemisphere it pushes southwards. The leading edge of this warm sector is a warm front and the trailing edge a cold front, the cold front moves in the same direction as the warm front but faster. When it catches up the warm front the pair become an occluded front.

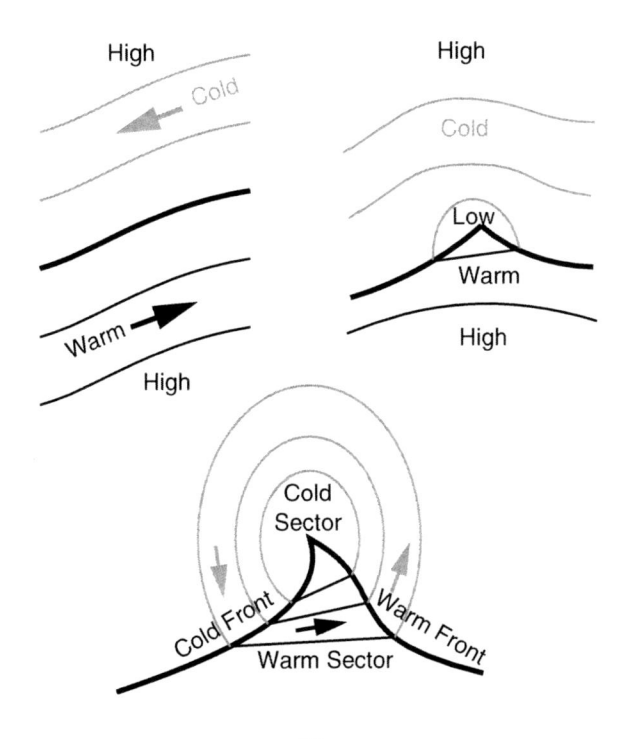

Cold front.

The colder air mass pushes itself under the warm sector ahead of it causing the warm air to rise. This lifting action of the cold front brings unstable weather, typically cumulus and cumulonimbus clouds with the associated wind and precipitation.

Following passage of the cold front the wind veers in the northern hemisphere, backs in the southern, the temperature and dew point temperature drop, and there is a rapid rise in pressure.

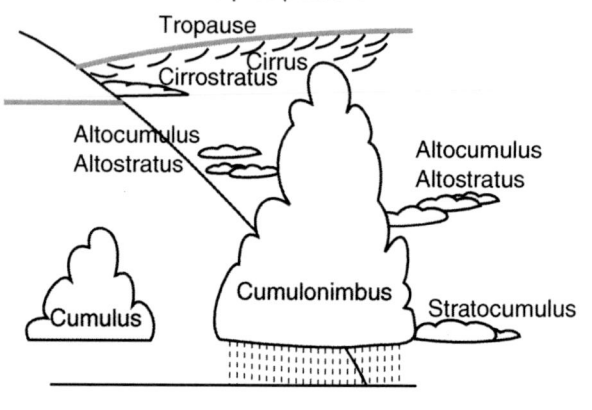

Warm front.

The warm front is the leading edge of the warm sector which rises up over the colder air ahead of it. As the warm front approaches the cloud will get lower and thicker until it reaches the ground. Precipitation will also increase from initially being virga, rain that does not reach the surface, to heavy rain or snow.

On frontal passage the wind will veer in the northern hemisphere, back in the southern, and the temperature and dew point temperature will rise. The clouds will change to low stratus and the pressure which was steadily falling ahead of the front will remain constant.

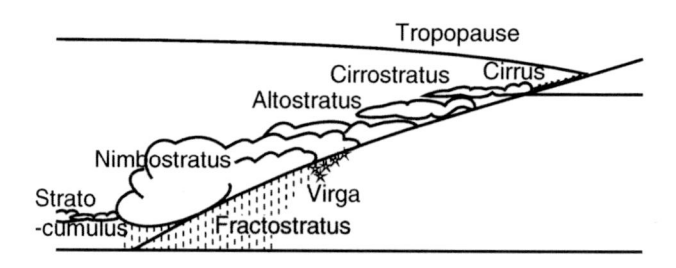

Occluded front.

When a cold front catches up a warm front, an occlusion results, if the air behind the cold front is cooler than that ahead of the warm front it is referred to as a cold occlusion, if it is warmer it is a warm occlusion.

The weather associated with an occlusion is a combination of that of a cold and warm front, there is a distinct possibility of there being embedded cumulonimbus clouds within the stratus.

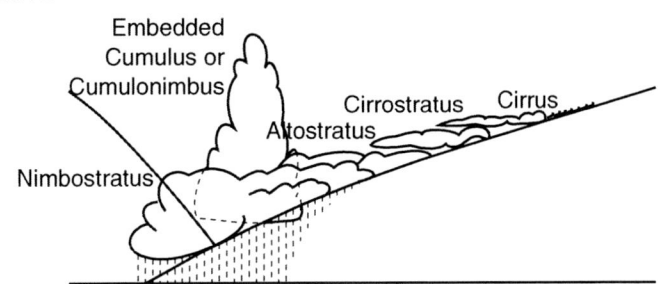

Stationary front.

A stationary front forms when the two opposing air masses are generating forces of a similar magnitude, the front may remain stationary for several days. The weather associated with a stationary front varies between that expected of a cold and warm front.

7

Winds.

Winds in the horizontal sense are described by the direction they are coming from and the wind speed, forecaster refer to true north for their wind directions where as ATC usually use magnetic north. When winds change direction, two common terms are used, if the wind direction changes in a clockwise direction it is said to have **veered**, whereas in an anticlockwise direction it is said to have **backed**.

Not only can winds change direction but it is not uncommon for the wind strength to also change. A sudden temporary increase in wind speed is called a **gust**, a **squall** is where this sudden change in wind speed lasts for several minutes and a **lull** is a decrease in wind speed.

Wind veers
clockwise change

Wind backs
anticlockwise change

The main cause of winds is the pressure difference between areas of high and low pressure. In an area of high pressure the air is experiencing subsidence, it is descending, and when it reaches the surface it diverges out away from the centre of high pressure. In an area of low pressure the air is converging towards the centre of the low and then it ascends. One would think this would lead to winds blowing directly from high to low, but this is not the case. Due to the earth's rotation this wind is deflected to the right in the northern hemisphere, to the left in the southern, this is known as Coriolis Effect. This causes the wind to actually blow parallel to the isobars, this is called the geostrophic wind, the closer the isobars the stronger the wind. In the northern hemisphere it blows anticlockwise around a low pressure area and clockwise around a high, whereas in the southern hemisphere these directions are reversed. This is Buys Ballot's law, with your back to the wind, the low pressure is on your left in the northern hemisphere and to the right in the southern hemisphere.

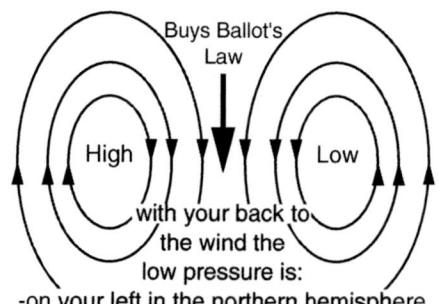

Buys Ballot's Law

High   Low

with your back to the wind the low pressure is:
-on your left in the northern hemisphere
-on your right in the southern hemisphere

13

Winds below 2,000 feet.

At the surface the winds tend to decrease in strength and blow slightly towards the area of low pressure due to surface friction. As one climbs up to 2,000 feet they increase, veering in the northern hemisphere but backing in the southern to blow parallel with the isobars.

Diurnal variations. These only affect winds below 2,000 feet as tabulated below.

These effects are due to the sun heating the ground in the day generating low level thermals

WIND	DAY TO NIGHT	NIGHT TO DAY
NORTHERN HEMISPHERE		
SURFACE	Backs and wind speed decreases	Veers and increases
1,000 FEET	Veers parallel to isobars and increases	Backs and decreases
2,000 FEET	No change	No change
SOUTHERN HEMISPHERE		
SURFACE	Veers and wind speed decreases	Backs and increases
1,000 FEET	Backs parallel to isobars and increases	Veers and decreases
2,000 FEET	No change	No change

which causes mixing with the faster moving 2,000 foot wind, resulting in higher surface winds by day.

Wind gradient. Is a term usually used by pilot's and describes the change in wind strength as an aircraft approaches to land.

Wind shear. Is a sudden change of wind direction or speed, it is at it's most dangerous when it occurs close to the ground.

Major airports have windshear detection equipment and all airports report expected or reported windshear experienced by other aircraft. Windshear can be expected in the vicinity of the following:

Thunderstorms and micro-bursts.

Mountain waves.

Large structures such as tall buildings.

Fronts.

Local winds.

These are winds that are generated by the effects of varying surface conditions.

Land and sea breezes.

These occur due to the different rate of heating, and cooling, of the sea and the coast.

A **land breeze** occurs at night due to the land cooling quicker than the sea, the air above the land cools and becomes more dense than the air over the sea so it flows away from the land.

A **sea breeze** occurs during the day, late morning or early afternoon, due to the land heating up quicker than the sea, this heats the air which becomes less dense than that over the sea, so the colder denser air from the sea flows in.

Mountain waves.

Some of the most turbulent winds occur when winds blow across mountain ranges. Mountain waves can form down wind of a mountain range for several hundred miles and are distinguished by lenticular clouds which remain stationary despite the strong horizontal airflow passing through them. At lower altitudes and closer to the mountains, again on the leeward side, rotor clouds may be formed, these must be avoided, they are extremely turbulent. When flying across a mountain range the pilot must be aware of the effects the peaks and valleys may have on the wind direction and strength in both the horizontal and vertical sense. Approaching the range from the wind ward side the pilot will experience updraughts, whereas crossing the range these will suddenly change to severe downdraughts, at full power the aircraft may not be able to maintain level flight. It is recommended when crossing a mountain range to remain 2,000 feet above the highest point and to not undertake the flight if forecast winds are above 20 knots. This is a very brief description of the winds affecting mountainous regions, if you are likely to operate in these environments there are several books written on the subject, and ensure you receive some dual instruction from an experienced instructor familiar with mountain flying.

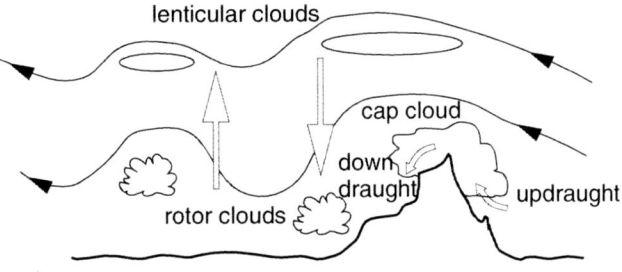

Fohn wind.

When orographic lifting from a mountain range has caused widespread rain on the windward side the air descending on the leeward side is unsaturated. Since it is unsaturated it warms as it descends at the dry adiabatic lapse rate and results in a warm wind blowing down the mountain, this is referred to as a **Fohn wind**.

Anabatic wind.

These form, during in the day, on south facing slopes being heated by the sun. As the sun heats the slope, the air above the slope is warmed by conduction and becomes less dense than the surrounding air and it rises up the slope.

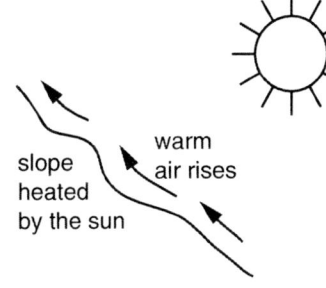

Katabatic wind.

These occur due to the cold slope cooling the air adjacent to it, this cold dense air then tumbles down the slope, these winds can reach gale force.

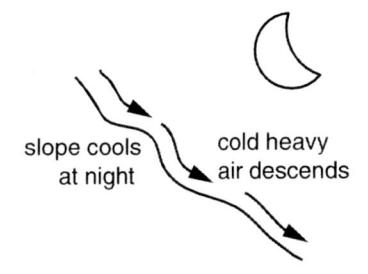

8

Clouds.

Clouds form when saturated air is cooled and excess water condenses out as water droplets or ice crystals. When these droplets become visible they form clouds. Clouds can be generally classified in two ways:

    The altitude they occupy.

    The shape of the cloud, either layered (stratus), or heaped (cumulus).

Cloud classification by altitude.

Clouds are classified by the altitude bands that they form in, these vary for different latitudes and are tabulated over the page.

Cloud classification by shape.

Clouds are either layered, of a stratus nature, or are heaped, of a cumulus nature. Certain clouds are a combination of both, i.e. stratocumulus. Stratus type clouds are usually associated with a stable atmosphere whereas cumulus are associated with instability.

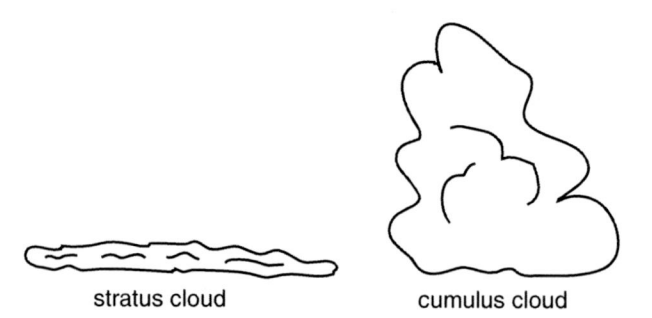

stratus cloud   cumulus cloud

Cloud Type by Altitude

FAMILY	CLASS	ABBREVIATION	ALTITUDE BANDS (feet)		
			TEMPERATE	POLAR	TROPICAL
HIGH CLOUD	Cirrus Cirrostratus Cirrocumulus	Ci Cs Cc	16,500 to 45,000	10,000 to 25,000	20,000 to 60,000
MEDIUM CLOUD	Altostratus Altocumulus	As Ac	6,500 to 23,000	6,500 to 13,000	6,500 to 25,000
LOW CLOUD	Nimbostratus Stratus Stratocumulus	Ns St Sc	Surface to 6,500	Surface to 6,500	Surface to 6,500
CLOUD OF EXTENSIVE VERTICAL DEVELOPMENT	Cumulus Cumulonimbus	Cu Cb	Near surface to 45,000	Near surface to 25,000	

Cloud formation.

As stated at the beginning of this chapter clouds form when saturated air is cooled and the excess water vapour condenses out as water droplets or ice crystals. The main reason the air is cooled is because of adiabatic cooling as a parcel of air ascends in the atmosphere. So cloud formation requires some form of lifting action; the four main lifting actions, the cloud types and precipitation associated with them are tabulated below.

TEMPERATURE CHANGE DUE TO	CLOUD TYPE	CLOUD NAME	SURFACE CHART SYMBOL	PRECIPITATION
Widespread ascent of air mass (Frontal activity)	Multilayer clouds	Cirrus Cirrostratus Altostratus Altocumulus Nimbostratus		Prolonged moderate rain and snow
Widespread irregular mixing of air	Low level layers or shallow layers of fog or cloud	Stratus Stratocumulus		Drizzle or possible light snow
Local convection currents	Cumuloform	Cumulus Cumulonimbus		Showers of rain, snow or hail. Possible thunderstorm activity
Local orographic disturbances	Lenticular or wave cloud	Lenticularis Rotor		Occassionaly an increase in existing precipitation

Frontal activity.

Frontal activity generates a wide-spread lifting action; cloud types and precipitation are dependant upon the type of front, this is discussed in more detail in the chapter on fronts.

Widespread irregular mixing of air.

This can occur when stable moist air in close proximity to the ground is subjected to a wind of about 10 knots. The wind causes the air adjacent to the ground to become turbulent and rise upwards, cooling adiabatically. The air, due to its high moisture content be-, comes saturated at low level forming cloud.

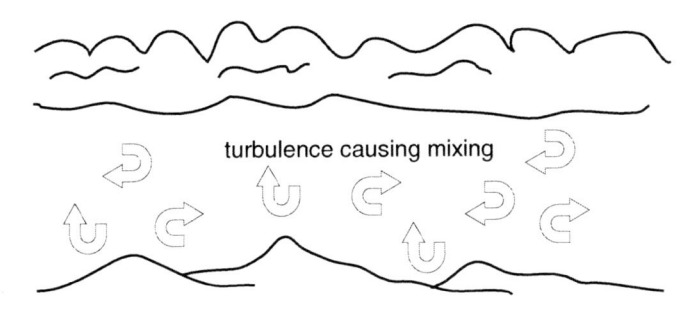

Local convection currents.

These form clouds of a cumulus nature, the bases of the clouds form where the temperature and dew point temperature are the same, in the case of fine weather cumulus clouds the tops form at the altitude where the cloud's temperature is the same as the surrounding air (stable). In the case of cumulonimbus and towering cumulus the air is unstable so the tops continue to rise and may reach 20,000 to 30,000 feet.

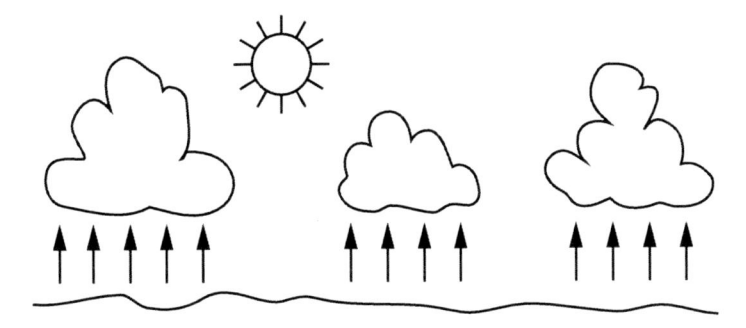

Local orographic disturbances.

This lifting action is due to the air being forced up by rising terrain such as a mountain range. As the air is forced up clouds form on the windward side of the mountain; further lifting will probably result in rain or snow falling. Once the air passes over the peak of the mountain it starts to descend. Since a large proportion of the moisture in the air has fallen as rain the air will become unsaturated at a higher altitude on the leeward side than on the windward side, the cloud base will therefore also be higher.

If the wind crossing the mountains is above 20 knots and approximately perpendicular to the range a mountain wave may form. This is distinguished by stationary lenticular clouds forming at regular intervals down wind of the range up to a distance of several hundred miles. Closer to the leeward side of the mountain at a lower level stationary roll clouds may form. These may look harmless but actually contain extremely turbulent air and flight in the vicinity of them must be avoided.

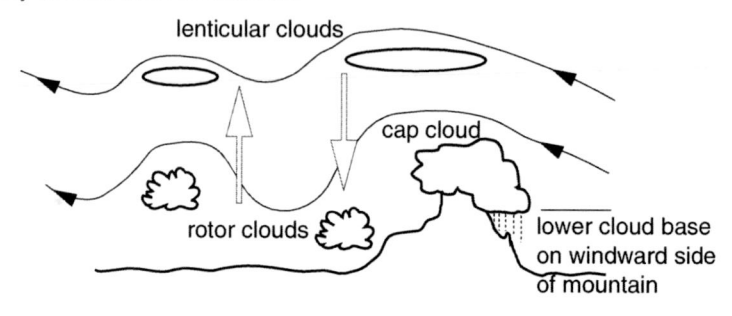

Calculation of cloud base.

It is possible to approximate the cloud base if the surface temperature and dew point temperature are known. Unsaturated air cools at the dry adiabatic lapse rate, namely 3 °C per 1,000 feet and the dew point decreases by 0.5 °C per 1,000 feet, so the two converge at 2.5 °C per 1,000 feet. If the surface temperature-dew point spread is only say 1.25 °C, the cloud base can be estimated at 500 feet.

9

Precipitation.

Precipitation occurs when the water droplets or ice crystals within a cloud become larger and heavy. The force of gravity overcomes any updraughts keeping them in the cloud and they fall to the surface.

Drizzle. Forms in humid air below stratus type cloud, the water droplets are very small and for them to fall from the cloud the updraughts must be very weak.

Rain. Is the most common form of precipitation and consists of large water droplets.

Snow. Is solid precipitation, usually in the form of snow flakes but it can fall as small solid pellets. Snow can fall with surface temperatures up to about 4^0 C.

Sleet. Is either a combination of rain and snow or snow that melts as it falls to the surface.

Hail. Is small pieces of ice falling usually from cumulonimbus clouds and thunderstorms. They can vary in size from a couple of millimetres up to the size of a tennis ball.

10

Thunderstorms.

Thunderstorms are one of the most violent meteorological phenomena that can cause even commercial airliners to alter their planned routing to avoid them.

Classification of thunderstorms.

Thunderstorms are classified by the lifting action that initially uplifts the air; this is either due to frontal activity or local air mass activity. In either case the air mass must have a high humidity and be unstable such that when the external lifting action is removed the thunderstorm continues to build.

Frontal activity.

Is usually associated with a cold front, the advancing cold air forcing its way under the warmer moist air causing it to lift. The line of thunderstorms forms along the front and moves with it.

Air mass activity.

Air mass thunderstorms form either due to local solar heating of the surface or due to the orographic lifting action of a mountain range. In both cases the thunderstorms tend to not move but remain in the local area.

Life cycle of thunderstorms.

Thunderstorms form when moist unstable air is lifted and forms a cumulonimbus cloud: the life cycle of this cloud is split into three stages:

    Development.
    Mature.
    Dissipation.

Development stage.

In the development stage smaller cumulus clouds join together forming a cumulonimbus cloud, with a diameter of up to five miles. Only updraughts exist in the cloud and as air rises within it, it entrains more air in from the surroundings. Even at this stage flight is not recommended through the cloud due to the high updraughts leading to turbulence.

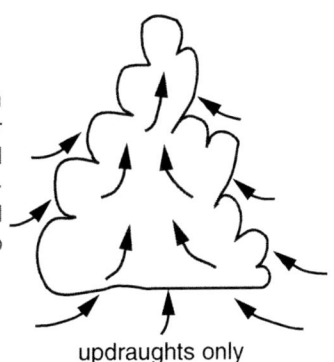

updraughts only

Mature stage.

The mature stage is signalled by the first precipitation falling from the cloud, there are now both strong updraughts and downdraughts. The top of the cloud will still be developing and air will still be entrained in from the surroundings. At the surface, along with the precipitation will come strong cold gusty winds and a lowering of the cloud base and visibility. If ice crystals are present in the cloud, the strong up and down draughts will cause various parts of the cloud to become positively and negatively charged. Lightning will occur if the potential difference between these charges becomes sufficient, lighting may remain in the cloud, be between clouds or go to the ground.

downdraughts and updraughts

Flight within a mature cumulonimbus cloud must be avoided due to severe turbulence from the strong up and down draughts. Flight in the vicinity of the cloud particularly at low level is not recommended due to the likelihood of severe gusts.

Dissipation stage.

The dissipation stage is signalled by the ice crystals in the top of the cloud being blown downwind in an anvil shape. At the surface the precipitation will decrease, the cloud base and visibility will rise. Within the cloud the updraughts will have almost ceased.

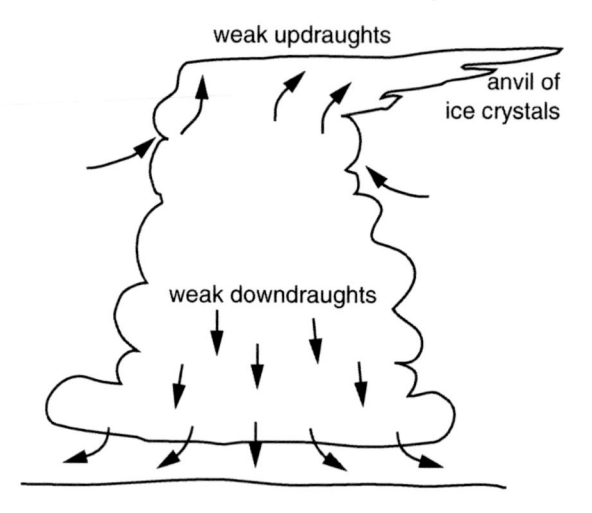

weak updraughts

anvil of ice crystals

weak downdraughts

Hazards associated with thunderstorms.

Turbulence. Due to the strong updraughts and down draughts within the cloud, extreme turbulence is likely to be experienced. This can be of a severity that will exceed the structural limits of the aircraft.

Hail. Large hail stones can form in the cloud. If flown through, these can damage radomes and the skin of the aircraft.

Cloud base. When the mature stage of development is reached the cloud base and surface visibility drop considerably.

Icing. Large supercooled water droplets are in abundance within a cumulonimbus cloud. These would lead to severe airframe (rime) and engine icing.

Lightning. Lightning presents two problems to aircraft: the sudden flash particularly at night can temporarily blind the pilot and secondly a direct hit on the aircraft could cause electrical or structural damage.

Micro-bursts. These are sudden local downdraughts from the base of the cloud; they hit the ground and spread out. They are of particular concern when taking off or landing. Let us consider the take off case. The pilot initiates the climb and is suddenly subjected to a strong head wind; the aircraft's indicated airspeed increases, the pilot slows the aircraft. The head wind suddenly changes to a downdraught and the airspeed is now low, also the aircraft is in a column of descending air, the rate of climb could be zero. The aircraft now experiences a tail wind. This could quite easily take the aircraft below the stall speed and it crashes. A similar outcome could be the result of approaching to land through a microburst.

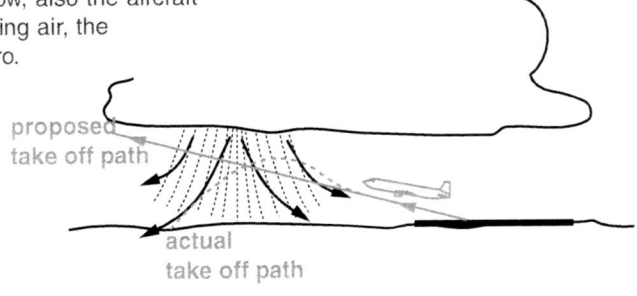

11

Fog and Reduced Visibility.

The one factor that can restrict all aviators, be they a private pilot or a Jumbo jet pilot, is fog or reduced visibility at the planned destination.

Reduced visibility can be due to:

    Heavy precipitation, i.e. a snow storm.

    Particles being blown up from the ground, i.e. a dust storm.

    Particles held in suspension, i.e. fog.

The first two are fairly self explanatory.

Fog.

The most problematic of the particles held in suspension is fog; the other common two, mist and haze, are more of an inconvenience and generally do not restrict flight operations too much. These are defined below:

    Fog is when the visibility drops below 1,000 metres.

    Mist is when the visibility is reduced to between 1,000 and 2,000 metres.

    Haze is reduced visibility due to small particles held in suspension; it can be particularly bad when there is an inversion and you are flying into the sun.

Advection fog.

Forms when moist air is moving over a colder surface, be it land or water. The air is cooled below its dew point temperature and fog forms, often over a large area. Advection fog will form in winds of up to 25 knots, it will only disperse, if the wind direction changes or the strength increases considerably, or by solar heating.

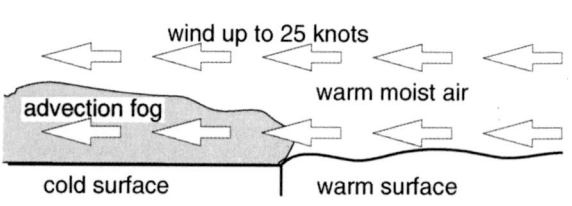

Radiation fog.

Forms on clear calm nights when the temperature dew point spread is small. The earth's surface cools, and by conduction cools the air in contact with it to below its dew point temperature and fog forms. If a light wind exists this will tend to mix the air adjacent to the ground with that above and the fog will thicken. Radiation fog is dispersed by either a wind of 10 knots plus or by solar heating.

clear night

light winds

radiation fog

Hill fog.

Hill fog is orographic cloud covering high ground. The lifting effect of the rising terrain allows the air mass to cool adiabatically and if cooled to below its dew point hill fog forms.

Frontal fog.

Forms when the rain falling from a warm front saturates the colder air below the front forming a band of fog just ahead of the front that moves with the front.

Freezing fog.

This is where the water droplets forming the fog are below freezing. Being very small droplets they freeze on impact and produce what is called rime ice. Rime ice is dealt with in the Icing chapter.

Vertical and oblique visibility.

A pilot over-flying an aerodrome that has reduced surface visibility due to fog or haze may, from an initial look down at the aerodrome, assume there will be no problem in landing there. However, on rolling out onto long finals the aerodrome that was visible a minute ago is now nowhere to be seen in the fog or haze. The pilot forgot that looking straight down on the aerodrome the thickness of fog may be only a few hundred feet where as on long finals the slant distance through the fog may be a mile or more.

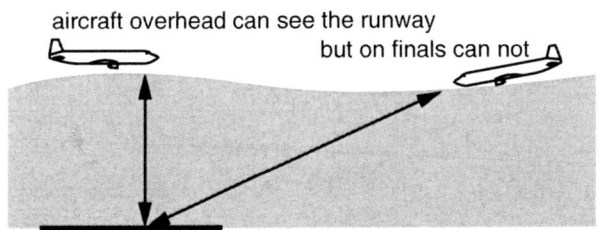

aircraft overhead can see the runway
but on finals can not

12

Icing.

Icing can be split into two distinct categories, airframe icing, either in flight or when parked, and engine icing, which in the case of a piston engine aircraft can occur on a bright cloud-free day.

Airframe icing.

The problem of airframe icing is twofold:

> The aerodynamics of the wings are affected increasing the drag and reducing the lift.
>
> The aircraft's weight is increased.

In both cases the aircraft's performance decreases and the engine(s) may have insufficient power to maintain the aircraft's altitude or under severe icing conditions maintain flight. An additional problem arises if the aircraft has an inefficient windshield heater in that the pilot can not see out.

The various types of airframe icing will now be discussed.

Clear ice

Clear ice forms when large water droplets freeze as they flow back over a surface such as a wing. These super cooled droplets are usually found in cumulus type cloud, by flowing over the surface their main detrimental effect is an increase in the aircraft's weight.

Rime ice.

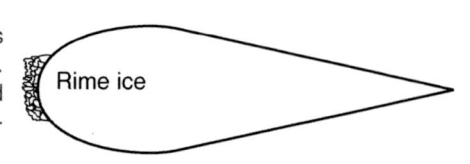

Rime ice forms when small water droplets freeze on impact trapping air between them. These small supercooled droplets are found in stratus type cloud or freezing fog. By instantaneously freezing on impact they build up on the leading edge of wings, horizontal and vertical stabilisers and have a detrimental effect on the aerodynamics of the aircraft. They have little effect in increasing the aircraft's weight.

Mixed or cloudy ice.

This is a combination of clear and rime icing and may be found in towering cumulus or clouds formed by orographic lifting.

Hoar frost.

This is the icing you find on your car the morning after a cold clear night; the same effect occurs on aircraft left out over night. The temperature of the surface is below freezing and has cooled the air in contact with it to below its dew point resulting in the moisture in the air condensing out as ice. This is the only form of structural icing that occurs when there is no visible moisture. In flight it occurs when an aircraft cruising at sub zero temperatures rapidly descends into warmer humid air. The aircraft's surface is still below freezing and the moisture condenses out as ice all over the aircraft, the most alarming aspect for the pilot is the sudden loss of visibility through the windshield.

Preflight actions.

Before flight the aircraft **must have all** ice and snow removed from it. Pay particular attention to the lift producing surfaces, the windshield and any hinges. The latter is extremely important because you could experience a control seizure making the aircraft unflyable.

In-flight actions.

Unless the aircraft is certified for known icing conditions do not fly in forecast icing conditions. Aircraft certified for flight in icing conditions have two types of icing protection:

> **De-Icing Equipment** is designed to remove ice that is present on the aircraft, this would include de-icing boots fitted to the leading edge of wings.
>
> **Anti-Icing Equipment** is designed to prevent icing occurring and would include heated windshields and engine anti-ice.

If you inadvertently enter icing conditions if possible do a 180^0 turn. If this is not feasible, and terrain clearance permitting, attempt to descend to warmer air or clear of cloud. If sufficient power is available attempt to climb through the icing layer. This option has the disadvantage that you will be carrying all that ice with you even after you leave the icing layer until you descend into warmer air that is above freezing.

Carburettor icing

Carburettor icing can occur when ambient temperatures are above freezing and the sky is clear. When air enters the venturi of the carburettor it accelerates, which causes its temperature to drop, in addition the fuel evaporates in the venturi causing the air temperature to drop further. If the combined effects of these bring the local air temperature to below 0 ^{0}C and there is moisture in the air it will condense out as ice. As this ice builds up it will make the venturi smaller until it becomes blocked and the engine stops producing any power. Note, in an aeroplane it is unlikely the engine will actually stop because the propeller will continue to windmill. This is not the case in a helicopter. To prevent this build up of ice, carburettor equipped aircraft have a system that diverts air across the hot exhaust system and warms it prior to entering the carburettor. This is the **carburettor heat**. The carburettor heat should be used as per the aircraft's flight manual. Different aircraft have totally different procedures.

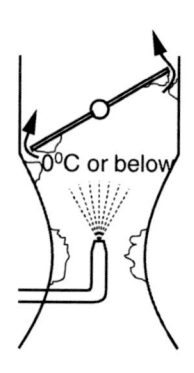

13

Climatology.

The global weather in very simple terms, neglecting local orographic effects, is due to the unequal heating of the earth's surface from the sun and the fact that the earth rotates about the poles. These simple assumptions lead to the following areas of high and low pressure, and wind directions.

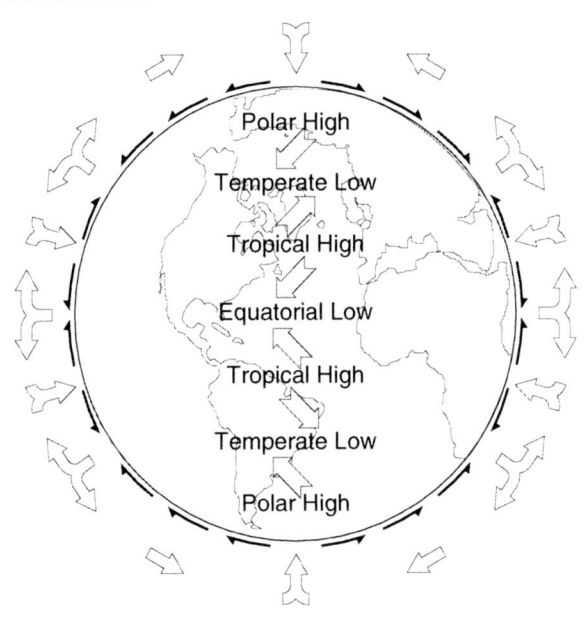

Polar High
Temperate Low
Tropical High
Equatorial Low
Tropical High
Temperate Low
Polar High

Europe.

The weather affecting Europe in the winter and summer is due to the influences of the polar front and the highs over Siberia and the Azores.

The upper winds all year round are predominantly westerly, in the winter veering to slightly north of west and backing in summer to slightly south of west.

Winter.

During the winter months the polar front moves southward and lies overhead south west England. Frontal depressions, originating in the Atlantic, travel in along the polar front giving rise to repetitive frontal activity across north west Europe, including the UK and Ireland. The prevailing surface winds are south westerly, often of gale force.

Eastern Europe and much of Scandinavia experiences cold cloudless anticyclonic weather due to the Siberian high and the associated ridge of high pressure stretching eastwards. Here the surface winds are easterly or north easterly.

The southern Mediterranean remains warm but experiences a few frontal depressions moving eastwards across the Mediterranean sea.

The freezing level is usually at the surface over northern Europe and Scotland rising to approximately 10,000 feet over the southern Mediterranean. Airframe icing is a hazard particularly in northern Europe with the repetitive frontal activity and associated cloud at all altitudes.

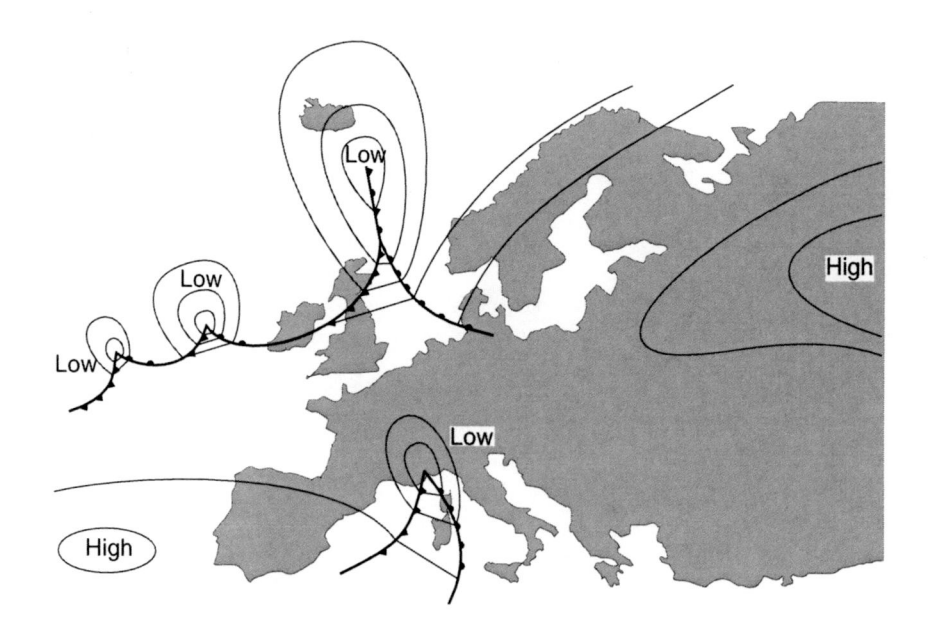

Summer.

During the summer the polar front moves northwards and lies overhead Scotland. The frontal depressions, forming in the Atlantic, are now less frequent and usually only affect north west Europe. Winds will normally be weaker than in the winter but gales will accompany some of the depressions. Occasionally a front will move down across the UK and Ireland.

The rest of Europe is affected by the ridge of high pressure stretching eastward from the Azores high. This leads to anticyclonic weather, slack winds and in coastal regions land and sea breezes predominate, in mountainous regions local orographic effects will predominate. Most cloud formation will be convective leading to fine weather cumulus and the occasional thunderstorm. Orographic lifting is likely in mountainous regions.

The freezing level in the summer is approximately 10,000 feet over northern Europe rising to approximately 15,000 feet over the southern Mediterranean.

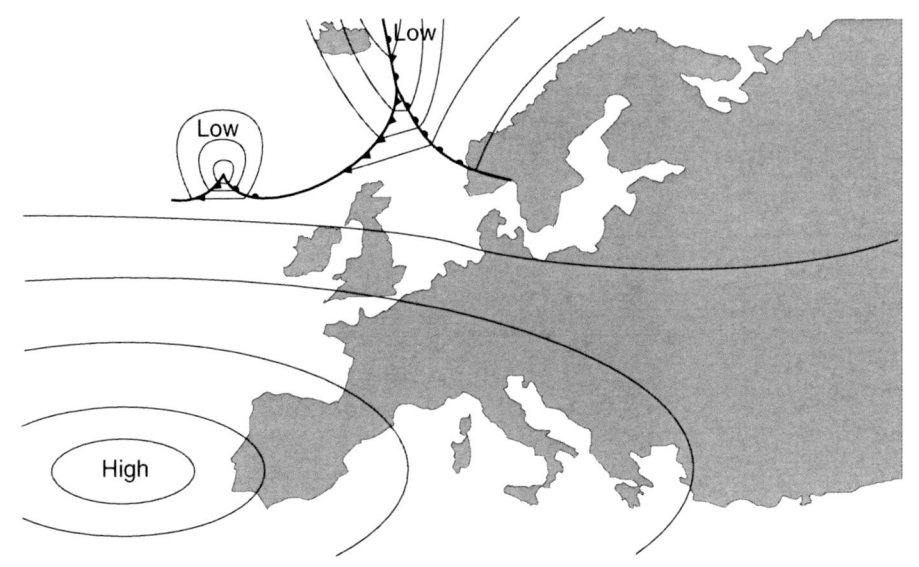

Flying in Europe.

The main problem pilots will experience flying in Europe, particularly in the winter is reduced visibility. In the case of frontal passage this will be due to snow or heavy rain and frontal fog. In the case of a warm sector this will be advection fog. Under anticyclonic conditions radiation fog may form at night which in the winter may not lift until early afternoon if at all.

In the summer conditions are much improved but occasionally frontal passage across high ground may result in some hill fog. Under anticyclonic conditions VFR flight may require more intense concentration than normal due to reduced visibility from haze, particularly when flying into the sun.

North America and Canada.

The weather affecting North America and Canada in the winter is due to the influences of the Atlantic and Pacific polar fronts, whereas in the summer it is the influences of the highs situated over Bermuda and the Pacific Ocean.

The upper winds all year round are predominantly westerly. In the winter in the vicinity of the jet stream these winds can exceed 100 knots and are associated with clear air turbulence, CAT.

Winter.

During the winter months the Atlantic polar front lies over southern Florida and the Pacific polar front lies over California. These result in coastal areas experiencing low ceilings, rain or snow. The east coasts weather is also affected by any depressions that have worked their way across the continent from the west.

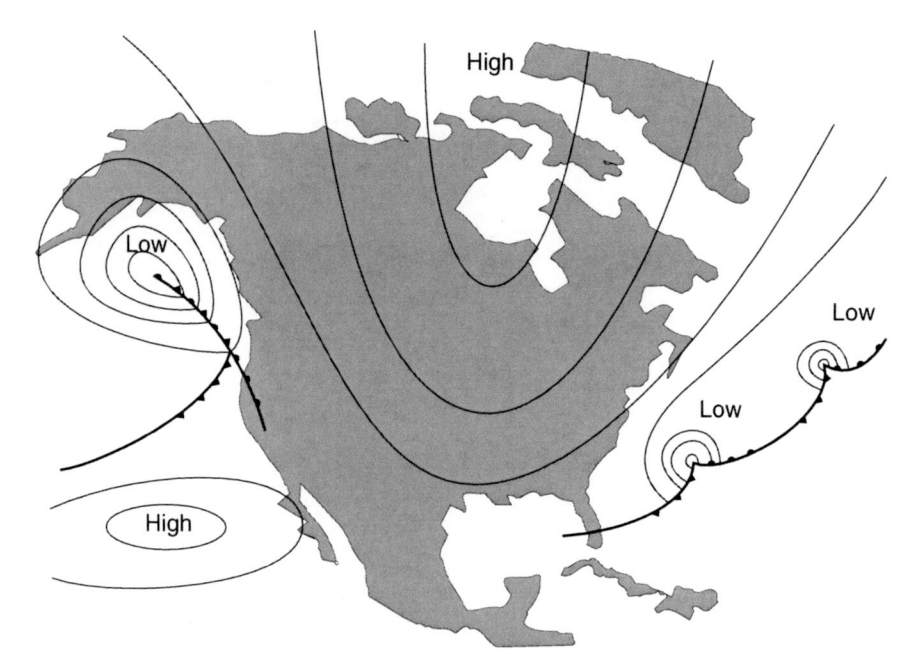

Warm fronts emanating from deep depressions forming off of Canada and the north eastern States of America bring deep snow and freezing rain to Canada and the northern States often resulting in the closure of airports. Away from the fronts these areas are affected by polar maritime air, and polar continental air that becomes moist and unstable as it crosses the Great Lakes, resulting in cold northerly winds, snow showers, icing and turbulence.

The central northern States of America are affected by depressions working their way across America from the west coast. On passage these will result in low ceilings and strong winds, but between the depressions flying conditions are good albeit very cold.

The surface and lower winds are dependant upon the position of frontal depressions; between depressions the winds are light and variable.

With the majority of mountain ranges orientated north-south the prevailing westerly winds will result in mountain waves forming downwind of the ranges when the winds are strong.

During the winter months the freezing level lies between the surface and 5,000 feet.

Summer.

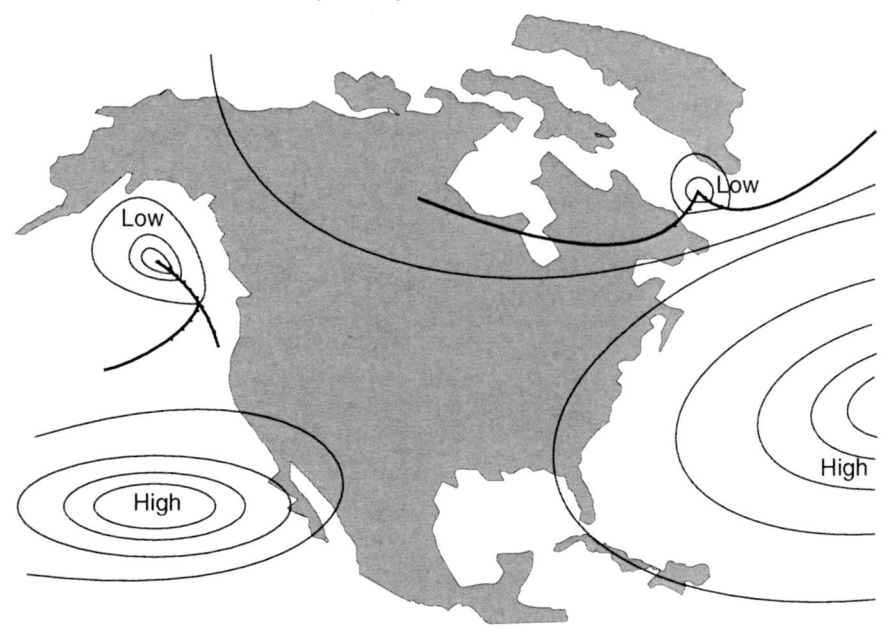

During the summer months the Atlantic and Pacific polar fronts move north and lie over Newfoundland and Alaska respectively. The weather is now predominantly affected by the high pressure regions centred over Bermuda and the Pacific Ocean. These anticyclonic conditions extend over the majority of north America giving rise to very favourable flying conditions.

Coastal regions, both east and west can experience advection fog being blown inland by sea breezes.

The eastern States, particularly in the region of Kansas and Missouri, experience tornadoes and severe thunderstorms that cause structural damage to buildings etc.

The surface and lower winds are south westerly over the eastern States and north westerly over the western States.

During the summer months the freezing level lies between 10,000 and 15,000 feet.

Australia.

The weather affecting Australia in January is due to the influences of the Inter-Tropical Convergence Zone,(ITCZ), and the equatorial low in the far north, and south of the ITCZ by the subtropical highs situated in the Indian and Pacific Oceans. In July the ITCZ and equatorial low move north leaving the two subtropical highs as the main influence, except in the south east and Tasmania which are affected by frontal activity associated with lows passing just south of Tasmania.

The upper winds all year round are predominantly westerly, but in January when the ITCZ moves over northern Australia the upper winds are easterly to the north of the ITCZ.

Coastal regions can be effected all year round by strong land and sea breezes.

January.

In January the equatorial low is centred over northern Australia, or just to the North. The ITCZ dips southwards and clips northern Australia. To the south of the ITCZ anticyclones move across the country in an easterly direction separated by troughs and cols drifting up from the south.

Weather to the north of the ITCZ is hot and humid with severe thunderstorms and squalls developing resulting in persistent downpours of rain and hail. Surface winds away from the thunderstorms and squalls are northerly or north westerly.

To the south of the ITCZ it is hot and turbulent with clear skies, although visibility is restricted by haze due to dust particles up to 10,000 feet. Further south severe turbulence can be expected over high ground. Surface winds are south easterly reducing to light and variable in the south east. However the south east can be affected by cold fronts resulting in severe dust storms, thunderstorms, turbulence, and on frontal passage, strong southerly winds locally referred to as the "Southerly Buster".

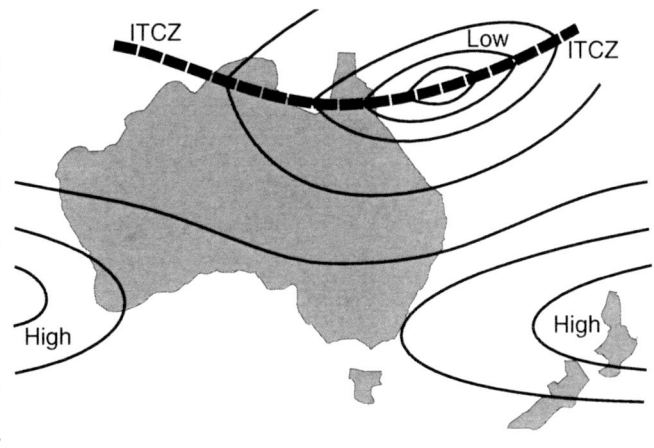

Both the north east and north west coastal areas may be affected by tropical revolving storms or hurricanes.

July.

The ITCZ has now moved well North leaving northern and central Australia to be influenced by the two subtropical highs. Within this band of high pressure anticyclones drift across the country from west to east. The weather is much the same as that experienced in January: hot, turbulent, with clear skies and haze up to 10,000 feet. Further south occasional frontal activity, due to depressions passing South of Tasmania, brings cloud and rain.

Surface winds are southerly or south easterly in the north decreasing to light variable in the south. The south east's winds are dependent upon any frontal activity, varying from a north westerly ahead of a warm front, backing through a westerly in the warm sector to a strong southerly on passage of the cold front. In mountainous regions these strong southerlies are likely to result in mountain waves.

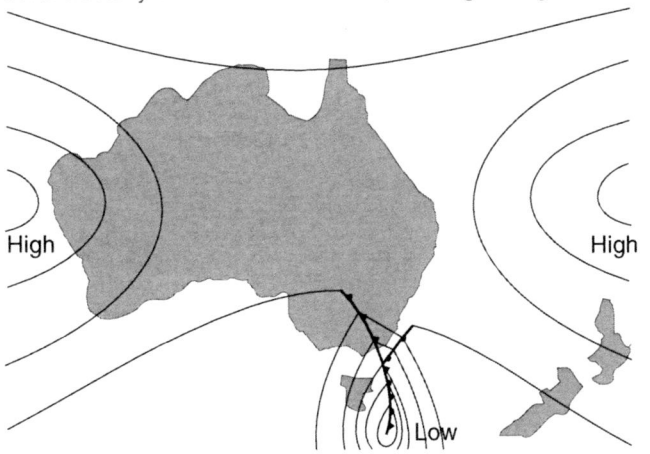

South Africa.

The weather affecting

South Africa in January is due to the ITCZ and the equatorial low, both situated just to the West of Madagascar, in the north, and in the south by the subtropical high over the Atlantic Ocean. In July the ITCZ and equatorial low move north leaving the subtropical high over the Atlantic and the similar high over the Indian Ocean as the main influences, except in the extreme south which is affected by frontal activity associated with lows passing just south of Africa.

January.

In January the equatorial low and the ITCZ are situated just to the north east of South Africa and bring with them the rainy season. Low stratus lingers all day, and as the day progresses towering cumulus and cumulonimbus form resulting in heavy showers. By the afternoon thunderstorms and squalls are beginning to form.

As one moves south the weather improves to fair weather cumulus with a slight chance of

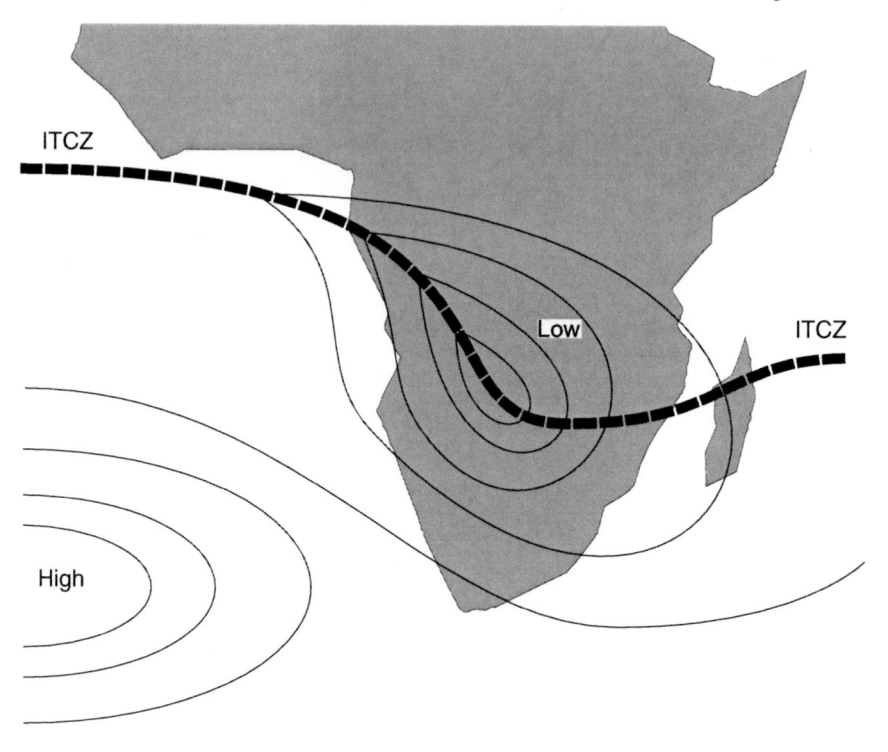

scattered thunderstorms in the evenings.

Surface winds are south easterly trade winds reducing to light and variable in the south where land and sea breezes predominate.

Upper winds are easterly around 25 knots to the north, but to the south they become a strong westerly due to the subtropical jet stream.

July.

In July the highs over the Atlantic and Indian oceans predominate and the dry season has arrived. Clear skies and haze due to dust are accompanied by very turbulent air. The southern tip of South Africa is affected by frontal activity associated with lows passing to the south.

Surface winds are variable; in the southern tip winds are dependent upon any frontal activity, varying from a north westerly ahead of a warm front, backing through a westerly in the warm sector to a strong southerly on passage of the cold front.

Upper winds are westerly, being fairly weak to the north but strengthening as one moves south into the influence of the subtropical jet stream.

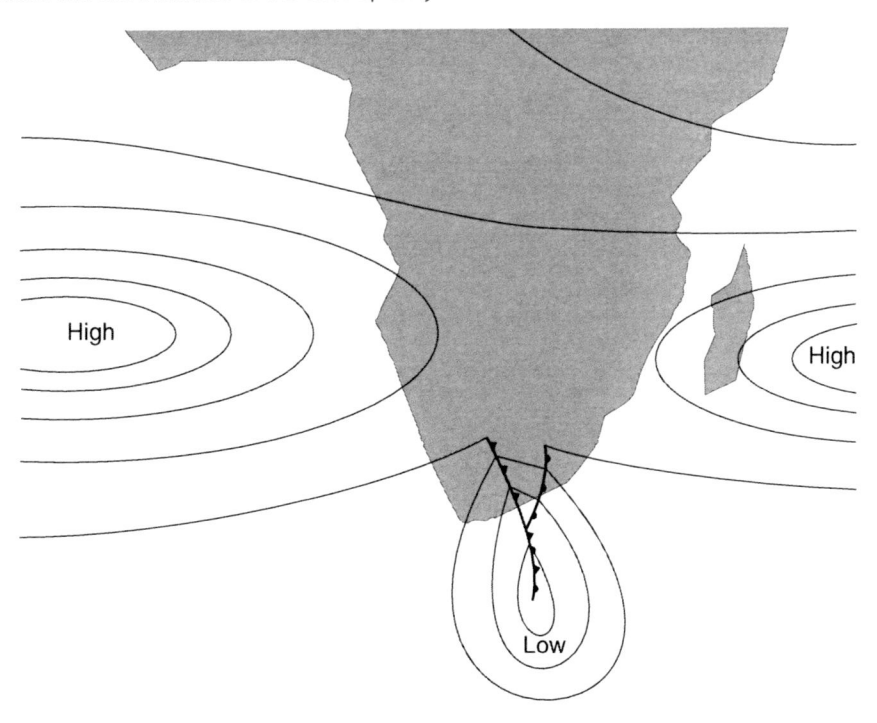

14

The Meteorological Organisation.

Aeronautical meteorological offices.

These are located at the Air Traffic Control Centres and at some of the larger civil aerodromes. Their responsibility is for the collection of the meteorological observations and the dissemination, world wide, of charts, forecasts and SIGMETs for their area and the aerodromes within it. For obvious reasons they are open 24 hours per day.

Aerodrome meteorological offices.

These are the meteorological offices based at aerodromes, they supply information received from the aeronautical meteorological offices to pilots. These offices may have a forecasting facility. Unlike the aeronautical offices, these may be open only at times that suit the operating hours of the aerodrome.

Meteorological services at aerodromes.

At aerodromes with a resident meteorological office pilot's can walk in and analyse the various charts and forecasts. Generally forecasters are not available for direct consultation, but at larger aerodromes they may be.

The large majority of small general aviation aerodromes have no meteorological office and rely on a faxed copy of the significant weather chart and local METARs and TAFs. More on these later.

Availability of periodic weather forecasts.

Weather forecasts are issued periodically, depending upon the type of forecast. TAFs are issued every 3 hours whereas significant weather charts are issued every 6 hours.

In the UK a recorded AIRMET service is available covering the low level weather over the UK by region. This is revised every 6 hours.

15

Weather Analysis and Forecasting.

Weather charts, symbols and signs.

The synoptic chart is the chart used by meteorologists to produce the significant weather charts issued to pilots for self briefings. The synoptic chart is a map with all the reporting stations marked on it, each reporting station's weather is marked in code around that station.

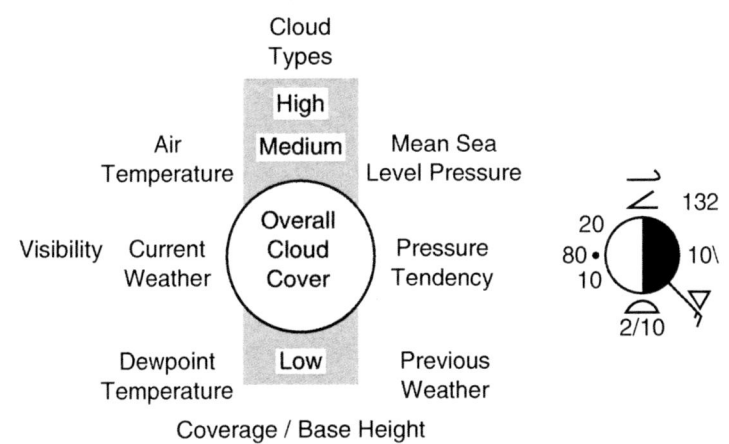

```
                    Cloud
                    Types

                    High
        Air         Medium      Mean Sea
        Temperature             Level Pressure

                    Overall
Visibility  Current Cloud       Pressure
            Weather Cover       Tendency

        Dewpoint    Low         Previous
        Temperature             Weather
                Coverage / Base Height
```

Surface Wind indicated by an arrow indicating direction
and tail feathers indicating strength

In the example on the right, the reporting station's weather is:

High Cloud is Cirrus.

Medium Cloud is Altostratus.

Low Cloud is Cumulus, with a coverage of $2/_8$ths and a base of 1,000 feet.

Overall Cloud cover is $4/_8$ths.

The air temperature and dewpoint are 20 °C and 10 °C respectively.

The current weather is intermittent light rain and the visibility is 30 km, (decoded below 50 by adding 00 and read as metres, above 50 deduct 50 and read as kilometres.)

The mean sea level pressure is 1013.2 hPa and has decreased 1 hPa in the last 3 hours.

The wind is 140 °T at 15 knots.

The previous weather was showers.

This chart shows actual weather conditions, the meteorologist then uses his skill and experience to produce the significant weather charts which are a forecast of what is expected to happen.

Prognostic charts for general aviation.

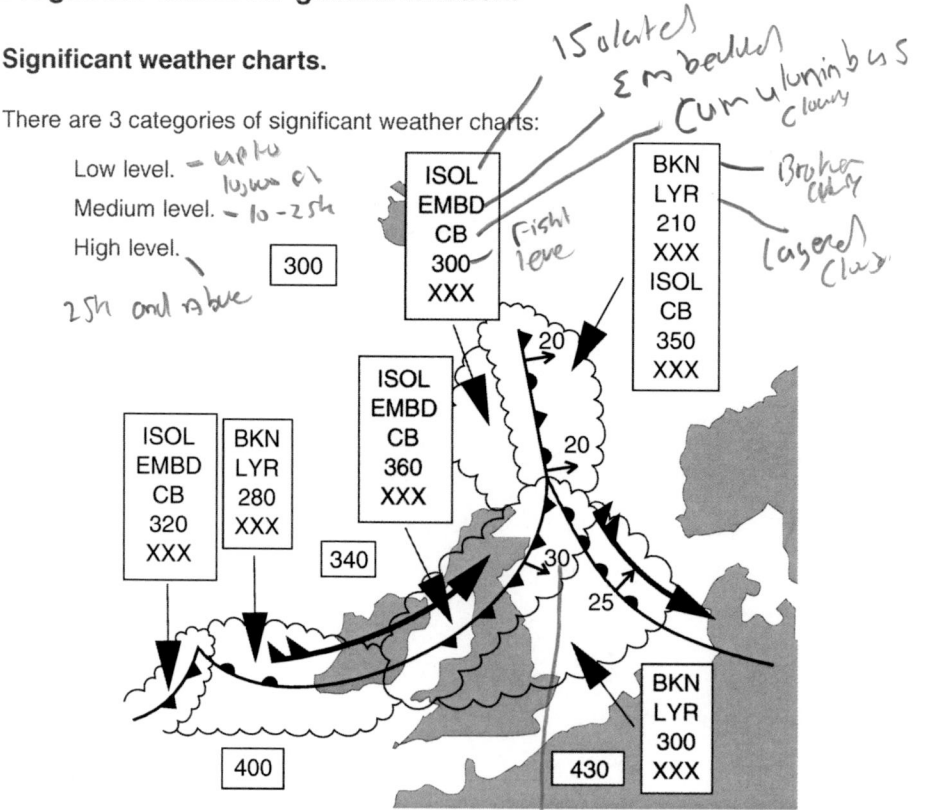

Significant weather charts.

There are 3 categories of significant weather charts:

Low level. — up to lower cl
Medium level. — 10 - 25k
High level. — 25k and above

Annotations: Isolated Embedded Cumulonimbus Clouds; Broken clouds; Layered Clouds; Fish level; Wind speed

Chart boxes:
- 300
- ISOL EMBD CB 300 XXX
- BKN LYR 210 XXX
- ISOL CB 350 XXX
- ISOL EMBD CB 320 XXX
- BKN LYR 280 XXX
- ISOL EMBD CB 360 XXX
- 340
- 400
- 430
- BKN LYR 300 XXX

Wind arrows: 20, 20, 30, 25

These charts are forecasts of the weather likely to occur for a period of 9 hours ahead, they are revised every 6 hours.

43

Charts indicating winds.

There are several charts issued showing the wind strength and direction at various altitudes. The most common for general aviation use is the spot wind and temperature chart indicating upper winds and temperatures for spot locations.

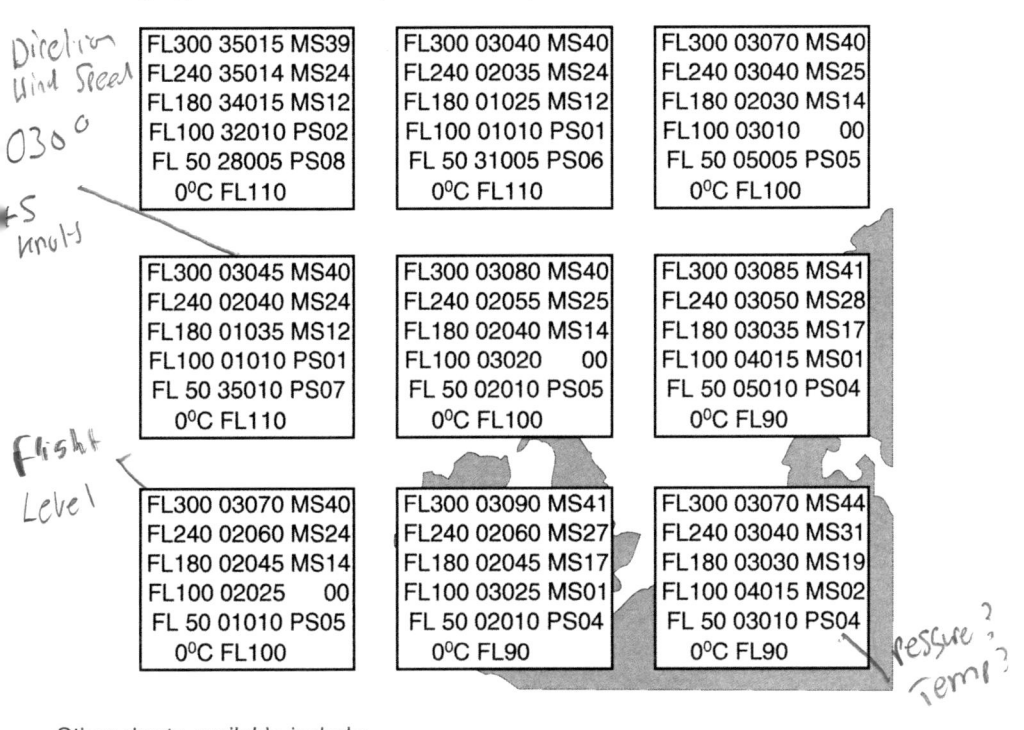

Direction *Wind Speed* 030° *5 knots*

Flight Level

FL300 35015 MS39	FL300 03040 MS40	FL300 03070 MS40
FL240 35014 MS24	FL240 02035 MS24	FL240 03040 MS25
FL180 34015 MS12	FL180 01025 MS12	FL180 02030 MS14
FL100 32010 PS02	FL100 01010 PS01	FL100 03010 00
FL 50 28005 PS08	FL 50 31005 PS06	FL 50 05005 PS05
0°C FL110	0°C FL110	0°C FL100

FL300 03045 MS40	FL300 03080 MS40	FL300 03085 MS41
FL240 02040 MS24	FL240 02055 MS25	FL240 03050 MS28
FL180 01035 MS12	FL180 02040 MS14	FL180 03035 MS17
FL100 01010 PS01	FL100 03020 00	FL100 04015 MS01
FL 50 35010 PS07	FL 50 02010 PS05	FL 50 05010 PS04
0°C FL110	0°C FL100	0°C FL90

FL300 03070 MS40	FL300 03090 MS41	FL300 03070 MS44
FL240 02060 MS24	FL240 02060 MS27	FL240 03040 MS31
FL180 02045 MS14	FL180 02045 MS17	FL180 03030 MS19
FL100 02025 00	FL100 03025 MS01	FL100 04015 MS02
FL 50 01010 PS05	FL 50 02010 PS04	FL 50 03010 PS04
0°C FL100	0°C FL90	0°C FL90

Pressure? Temp?

Other charts available include:

Contour-isotach chart indicating points of constant wind speed at the charts level.

Wind-temperature chart indicating winds and temperatures at the charts level.

16

Weather Information for Flight Planning.

The meteorological service can supply the pilot with various types of information on the current weather and forecast weather for the route to be flown: this information comes in several formats.

Most major aerodromes have forecasts produced, called TAFs, indicating the expected weather at the aerodrome for a given time period, usually 9 hours ahead.

Reports of the actual weather at the aerodrome are also available, called METARs. These are taken on the hour and half past the hour. Special observations are taken if the weather changes dramatically between standard observations.

Various meteorological charts, mentioned previously, are available showing typically the surface weather and the winds aloft expected for the forecast period.

The meteorological office requires prior notice to prepare a folder of weather information for a planned flight: typically this is 4 hours for a flight of 500 nm or more and 2 hours for less.

Reports and forecasts for departure.

The departure aerodrome is likely to have both a METAR and a TAF covering the expected time of departure. The METAR can not only be used to see the current weather but to judge whether the forecast appears correct. If departing from an aerodrome without any reporting facilities it is probable there will be an aerodrome fairly local that will have reporting facilities. These METARs and TAFs will indicate to the pilot the prevailing weather.

En-route, destination and alternate(s).

Similar to the departure aerodrome, the destination and alternates are likely to have METARs and TAFs. The en-route phase of the flight can be assessed from both significant weather charts, and for low level flights, TAFs of aerodromes along the route.

Interpretation of coded information.

The information available from the meteorological office, either directly or through print-outs at aerodromes is in code. These codes use the same decodes for the presentation of weather information but a few differences arise with regard to the presentation of time.

METARs. — Weather Reports

At major airports routine weather reports (METARs), are taken every half hour. If a significant change in weather occurs between routine reports a special report is issued. METARs are in a standard format and contain the following information in the order listed:

- Aerodrome Identifier.
- Surface Wind.
- Visibility.
- Runway Visual Range, if applicable.
- Current Weather.
- Cloud or, when applicable, vertical visibility.
- Air Temperature and Dew Point Temperature.
- Pressure, QNH.
- Supplemental Information, if appropriate.
- Trend.

METARs are decoded as follows:

METAR	EINN 1100Z 18010G20KT 150V210	500	R24/0400	-SHSN
BKN005	OVC010 01/00 Q0985 REFZRA	NOSIG=		

METAR   EINN 1100Z

Routine weather report for Shannon Airport at 1100 UTC.

A Special weather report would use **SPECI** instead of **METAR**.

18010G20KT 150V210

Surface wind relative to True North, wind is blowing from **180 °True**, at **10 knots Gusting** to **20 knots**, the wind direction is **varying** between **150 °** and **210 °True**. If winds are light and **variable, VRB** will be used.

500

Minimum Visibility is **500 metres**: if visibility is greater than **10 km**, **9999** will be used. In the case where visibility in one direction is below **1500 m** and in another is greater than **5,000 m** both will be given followed by the appropriate true directions, **1000S 7000N**.

R24/0400

The Runway Visual Range at the touch down zone of runway **24** is **400 metres**.

-SHSN

The present weather is **- light, SH, showers** of, **SN, snow**. Tabulated below are the present weather decodes.

BKN005   OVC010

COVERAGE		TYPE OF WEATHER		
INTENSITY OR LOCATION	**DESCRIPTION**	**PRECIPITATION**	**VISIBILITY**	**OTHER**
- Light	BC Patches	DZ Drizzle	BR Mist	DS Duststorm
Moderate (default)	BL Blowing	GR Hail	DU Wide spread dust	FC Funnel clouds
+ Heavy	DR Low drifting	GS Snow pellets or small hail	FG Fog	
VC with in the vicinity	FZ Supercooled	IC Suspended small ice particles	FU Smoke	PO Well developed dust or sand whirls
	MI Shallow	PE Ice pellets	HZ Haze	
	SH Showers	RA Rain	SA Sand	SQ Squalls
	TS Thunderstorm	SG Snow grains	VA Volcanic ash	SS Sandstorm
		SN Snow		

Cloud cover is **broken** at **500 feet**, **overcast** at **1,000 feet**.

The various decodes and their meanings are:

    SCT   scattered   1-4 oktas of sky is covered
    BKN broken   5-7 oktas of sky is covered

OVC overcast whole of sky is covered

CAVOK visibility greater than 10 km.

No cloud below 5000 feet, or the highest minimum sector altitude, which ever is lowest.

No cumulonimbus.

No precipitation, fog, thunderstorms or drifting snow, these are the most significant.

The cloud type is only mentioned if it is either **Cumulonimbus, CB,** or **Towering Cumulus, TCU.**

01/00

The outside air temperature is **+1⁰ C**, and the dew point temperature is **0⁰ C**. A minus temperature is indicated by an **M**, i.e. **M01** indicates **minus 1⁰ C**. Note, when the temperature and dew point temperature are within about 1⁰ C or less there is a good possibility of fog.

Q0985

The **QNH** is **0985 hectopascals**: if the QNH is given in inches it will be preceded by an **A** instead of the **Q**.

REFZRA

Recent weather, **FZ, freezing, RA, rain**. Certain aerodromes may report windshear if reported below 1600 feet above the aerodrome.

NOSIG

The trend is for **no significant change**. The other possible decodes being:

BECMG Becoming followed by the time span and details.

TEMPO Temporarily followed by the time span and details.

TAFs

TAFs unlike METARs are a forecast of the weather to be expected at an aerodrome over a given period. TAFs are in a standard format and contain the following information in the order listed:

Identification.
Surface Wind.
Visibility.
Weather.

Cloud, or when applicable vertical visibility.

Significant changes.

TAFs are decoded, using in most cases the same abbreviations as for METARs, as follows:

TAF   EINN 310900Z   1019   TEMPO   1216 7000 SHRA BKN010=

TAF   EINN 310900Z   1019

This is the Aerodrome forecast for Shannon, issued on the **31**st day of the month at **0900 UTC**, covering the period **1000 UTC** to **1900 UTC**.

18010G20KT 9999   BKN050

This decodes as per the METAR, a southerly wind of 10 knots gusting to 20 knots with a visibility of 10 km plus and broken cloud at 5,000 feet. If the sky is forecast to be clear this is indicated by **SKC**. This is the weather for the forecast period, if there are likely to be changes either of a temporary or permanent nature these will follow giving the expected time periods.

TEMPO   1216   7000   SHRA BKN010

In this case there is forecast to be a **temporary** change, between **1200 UTC** and **1600 UTC**, where the visibility will drop to **7,000 m**, in **moderate rain showers** and the broken cloud will be down to **1,000 feet**.

Where the forecaster is unsure of the likelihood of a certain meteorological event happening the probability is expressed as follows:

PROB 40   1315   +SHSN   OVC003

Between **1300 UTC** and **1500 UTC** there is a **40%** chance of **heavy snow showers** bringing the **visibility** and **ceiling** down to **500 m** and **300 feet** respectively.

When a TAF has been amended this is indicated by the code **AMD** preceding the aerodrome identifier.

Availability of ground reports for surface conditions.

At tower controlled aerodromes and some aerodromes with an advisory service the following are reported:

Current surface winds.

Windshear, either from detection equipment or when reported by other aircraft.

Visibility, when below VFR minimums, either that observed by the tower or from detection equipment, IRVR.

In the case of a tower controlled aerodrome these are usually official observations, in the case of an advisory service they are usually unofficial.

In flight meteorological information.

VOLMET.

Meteorological information is available to aircraft in flight on either HF or VHF transmissions; the VHF broadcasts are referred to as VOLMET's. These include plain language reports of the actual weather at local international airports.

ATIS.

At major airports a recorded message is available listing the airport's weather and other information affecting aircraft about to depart or arrive. This broadcast is referred to as an ATIS, there may be one for departures and a separate one for arrivals.

SIGMET.

These are reports to all aircraft of meteorological phenomena that may affect the safety of flight, they include:

Lines of thunderstorms.

Severe turbulence.

Severe icing.

These SIGMET's are broadcast by ATC on the frequencies appropriate for the areas affected; they are also available when the pilot is obtaining his preflight brief.

Glossary of terms.

Advection. Is where heat transfer occurs due to the horizontal movement of the air, i.e. advection fog.

Air mass. An extensive area of air whose moisture and temperature in the horizontal plane are the same, i.e. polar continental which is cold and dry.

Buys Ballot's law. When in the northern hemisphere with your back to the wind the area of low pressure is on your left and the area of high pressure on your right. Note in the southern hemisphere the reverse is the case.

Col. An area bounded by two areas of low pressure and two areas of high pressure. Typical weather associated with a Col is light and variable winds, low cloud and fog in the winter while in the summer expect mist lifting to form large cumuloform clouds, possibly thunderstorms.

Conduction. Is heat transfer due to bodily contact, i.e. the earth's surface cools and heats the lower atmosphere by conduction.

Convection. Is heat transfer within an air mass by the motion of that air mass, usually in the vertical sense, i.e. a warm convective up draught, in an unstable air mass, can lead to the development of a thunderstorm.

Convergence. Is the inflow of surface air towards the centre of a low pressure area.

Coriolis effect. Causes winds to blow parallel to the isobars instead of from high pressure to low. Winds blow clockwise around a high and anti-clockwise around a low in the northern hemisphere.

Dew point. This is the temperature to which an air mass has to be cooled for it to become saturated, the moisture in the air condenses out as liquid water droplets typically as clouds.

Diurnal variation. This is the difference in the day time air temperature and that at night.

Divergence. Is the outflow of surface air away from the centre of a high pressure region.

Fog. Is surface based cloud where the horizontal visibility is less than 1,000 metres, this cloud is formed of either water droplets or ice crystals.

Geostrophic wind. Is the wind blowing parallel to the isobars.

Gust. A sudden and brief change of wind speed.

Humidity. Is a measure of the moisture content of air. **Absolute Humidity** is air that is saturated with water vapour, it has a relative humidity of 100%, i.e. if there was any more water vapour present it would condense out as liquid water droplets, typically cloud.

Relative Humidity is the actual amount of water vapour in a parcel of air as a percentage of the maximum amount that parcel can hold with it condensing out as water.

Insolation. Is a measurement of the suns radiation.

International Standard Atmosphere. At sea level, a pressure of 1013.25 hPa, a density of 1225 grams per cubic metre and a temperature of +150 C. The temperature decreasing by 1.980 C per thousand feet of altitude to a temperature of -56.50 C at 36,000 feet, above which it remains constant up to 65,000 feet.

Isobar. A line drawn on a synoptic chart representing a constant pressure.

Isotach. A line showing constant wind speed.

Latent heat. Is the heat absorbed when either liquid water or ice changes to water vapour.

Line Squall. A narrow band of thunderstorms forming ahead of a cold front.

Mist. Is similar to fog but the visibility is greater than 1,000 metres.

QFE. Is an altimeter setting that indicates height above a fixed reference point, this is normally an aerodrome.

QNE. Is where the altimeter is set to 1013 hPa, this indicates the aircraft's vertical position with regard to a datum pressure of 1013 hPa and is referred to as Flight Level it is used by aircraft flying at higher altitudes.

QNH. Is an altimeter setting that indicates altitude above mean sea level, this is usually used to guarantee terrain clearance.

Radiation. Is the transfer of heat by electro magnetic waves, i.e. the sun heats up the earth by radiation.

Sigmet. Is a meteorological warning, to **all** pilots of **all** aircraft, of severe weather.

Squall. A sudden increase of wind speed of 15 knots or more.

Stratosphere. The shell of the atmosphere above the tropopause which is characterised by its constant temperature.

Sublimation. A term used to describe the change of ice directly to water vapour or vice versa.

Subsidence. Is the adiabatic heating of air as it sinks from a high altitude to a lower one.

Temperature Inversion. An increase of temperature with altitude.

Tropopause. The layer separating the troposphere from the stratosphere.

Troposphere. The inner shell of the atmosphere in contact with the earth's surface.

Volmet. A recorded message giving the weather conditions at several aerodromes transmitted on a HF or VHF frequency, i.e. Dublin Volmet on 127.0 Mhz.

Climatology.

The global weather in very simple terms, neglecting local orographic effects, is due to the unequal heating of the earth's surface from the sun and the fact the earth rotates about the poles. These simple assumptions lead to the following areas of high and low pressure, and wind directions.

Europe. The weather affecting Europe in the winter and summer is due to the influences of the polar front and the highs over Siberia and the Azores.

The upper winds all year round are predominantly westerlies, in the winter veering to slightly north of west and backing in summer to slightly south of west.

Winter. During the winter months the polar front moves southward and lies overhead south west England. Frontal depressions, originating in the Atlantic, travel in along the polar front giving rise to repetitive frontal activity across north west Europe, including the UK and Ireland. The prevailing surface winds being south westerly often of gale force.

Eastern Europe and much of Scandinavia experiences cold cloud less anticyclonic weather due to the Siberian high and the associated ridge of high pressure stretching eastwards. Here the surface winds are easterly or north easterly.

The southern Mediterranean remains warm but experiences a few frontal depressions moving eastwards across the Mediterranean sea.

The freezing level is usually at the surface over northern Europe and Scotland rising to approximately 10,000 feet over the southern Mediterranean. Airframe icing is a hazard particularly in northern Europe with the repetitive frontal activity and associated cloud at all altitudes.

Summer. During the summer the polar front moves northwards and lies overhead Scotland. The frontal depressions, forming in the Atlantic, are now less frequent and usually only affect north west Europe. Winds will normally be weaker than in the winter but gales will accompany some of the depressions. Occasionally a front will move down across the UK and Ireland.

The rest of Europe is affected by the ridge of high pressure stretching eastward from the Azores high. This leads to anticyclonic weather, slack winds and in coastal regions land / sea breezes predominate, in mountainous regions local orographic effects will predominate. Most cloud formation will be convective leading to fine weather cumulus and the occasional thunderstorm, orographic lifting is likely in mountainous regions.

The freezing level in the summer is approximately 10,000 feet over northern Europe rising to approximately 15,000 feet over the southern Mediterranean.

Flying in Europe. The main problem pilot's will experience flying in Europe, particularly in the winter is reduced visibility. In the case of frontal passage this will be due to snow or heavy rain and frontal fog, in the case of a warm sector this will be advection fog. Under anticyclonic conditions radiation fog may form at night which in the winter may not lift until early afternoon if at all.

In the summer conditions are much improved but occasionally frontal passage across high ground may result in some hill fog. Under anticyclonic conditions VFR flight may require more intense concentration than normal due to reduced visibility from haze, particularly when flying into the sun.

Index

A

Absolute Humidity 52
Adiabatic 5, 6, 8, 9, 16, 19, 20, 21
Advection 27, 51
Advection Fog 27, 34, 51
Aerodrome Meteorological Offices 41
Aeronautical Meteorological Offices 41
Air Mass 7, 10, 23, 51
Airframe Icing 29, 33
AIRMET 41
Altimeter 3
Altimetry 3–5
America 35
Anabatic Winds 16
Anti-Icing Equipment 30
Anticyclone 8
ATIS 50
Atmosphere 1–3
   Composition 1
Australia 37

B

Back 13
Buys Ballot's Law 13, 51

C

Canada 35
Carburettor Icing 31
CAT 35
CAVOK 48
Clear Air Turbulence 35
Clear Ice 29
Climatology 32–41
Cloud Base 21, 25
Cloud Classification
   By Altitude 17
   By Shape 17
Cloud Formation 19

Clouds 17–22
   Lenticular 15
   Roll 21
   Rotor 15
Cloudy Ice 30
Col 9, 51
Cold Front 11, 12, 23
Conduction 2, 16, 28, 51
Contour-Isotach Charts 44
Convection 20, 51
Convergence 9, 51
Coriolis 13, 51

D

DALR 5
De-Icing Equipment 30
Depression 9
Dew Point 51
Dew Point Temperature 20, 21, 27, 28
Diurnal Variations 14, 51
Divergence 8, 51
Drizzle 22

E

ELR 5
Engine Icing 25, 31
Environmental Lapse Rate 5
European Climate 32

F

Fog 27–29, 51
   Advection 27
   Freezing 28
   Frontal 28
   Hill 28
   Radiation 28
Fohn Wind 16
Freezing Fog 28
Freezing Level 33, 34, 52
Frontal Fog 28

Fronts 10–13
  Cold 11
  Fog 28
  Formation of 10
  Occluded 12
  Polar 32, 35, 36
  Stationary 12
  Warm 11

G

Geostrophic Wind 13, 52
Gust 13, 52

H

Hail 22, 25
Haze 8, 27, 28, 35
High
  Atlantic 39
  Azores 32
  Bermuda 35
  Indian 37, 39
  Pacific 35, 37
  Siberia 32
High Pressure 8
Hill Fog 28
Hoar Frost 30
Humidity 7, 23, 52
  Absolute 52
  Relative 52
Hurricanes 38

I

ICAO 2, 4
Icing 25, 29–32
  Carburettor 31
  Clear 29
  Cloudy or Mixed 30
  Engine 31
  Hoar Frost 30
  Rime 29
Insolation 52
Instability
  Absolute or Total 6
Instrumented Runway Visual Range 53

Inter-Tropical Convergence Zone 37, 52
International Civil Aviation Organisation 2
International Standard Atmosphere 2, 52
Inversion 7, 27, 53
IRVR 53
ISA 2
Isobar 13, 52
Isotach 52
ITCZ 37, 39, 52

J

Jet Stream 35, 40, 52

K

Katabatic Winds 16

L

Land Breeze 15
Lapse Rate
  Dry Adiabatic 5
  Environmental 5
  Pressure 2
  Saturated Adiabatic 5
Latent Heat 52
Lenticular Clouds 15, 21
Lightning 24, 25
Low Pressure 9

M

METAR 41, 45, 46
Meteorological Forecasts 41
Meteorological Organisation 41–42
Micro-bursts 15, 26
Mist 27, 52
Mixed Ice 30
Mountain Waves 15, 21

N

Nitrogen 1

O

Oblique Visibility 28
Occluded Front 12
Occlusion 12
Orographic Clouds 28
Oxygen 1
Ozone 1

P

Polar Front 32
Precipitation 22–23

Q

QFE 3, 52
QNE 4, 52
QNH 3, 53

R

Radiation 2, 52, 53
Radiation Fog 28, 34
Rain 22
Relative Humidity 52
Ridge 8
Rime Ice 28, 29
Roll Cloud 21
Rotor Cloud 15
Runway Visual Range 53
RVR 53

S

SALR 5
Saturated Air 5, 17, 19
Sea Breeze 15
SIGMET 41, 50, 53
Significant Weather Charts 43
Sleet 22
Snow 22
South Africa 39
Southerly Buster 38
Spot Wind Charts 44
Squall 13, 52, 53
Stability 5–7
   Absolute or Total 5

Standard Atmosphere 2, 52
Stationary Front 12
Stratosphere 1, 53
Sublimation 53
Subsidence 8, 13, 53
Super Cooled Droplets 29

T

TAF 41, 45, 48
Temperature 2, 52, 53
Thunderstorms 7, 15, 23–27
   Classification of 23
   Development 24
   Dissipation 25
   Hazards 25
   Life Cycle 23
   Mature 24
Tornadoes 37
Tropical Revolving Storms 38
Tropopause 1, 53
Troposphere 1, 53
Trough 9
Turbulence 24, 25

U

Upper Winds 32, 44

V

Veer 13
Vertical Visibility 28
Virga 11
Visibility 27, 28, 30, 34
   Oblique or Vertical 28
VOLMET 50, 53

W

Warm Front 11
Warm Sector 11
Weather Charts 42
   Contour-Isotach 44
   Significant 43
   Spot Wind 44
   Wind-Temperature 44

Weather Forecasts 41
  Prior Notice Required 45
Wind Gradient 14
Wind Shear 14
Wind-Temperature Charts 44
Winds 13–17
  Anabatic 16
  Backed 13
  Below 2,000 Feet 14
  Diurnal Variations 14
  Fohn 16
  Geostrophic 13
  Katabatic 16
  Prevailing 32
  Upper 32
  Veering 13